FACE READING

THE MUTE LANGUAGE

by

Arti Sharma

GOODWILL PUBLISHING HOUSE®
B-3 RATTAN JYOTI, 18 RAJENDRA PLACE
NEW DELHI -110008 (INDIA)

Published by
GOODWILL PUBLISHING HOUSE®
B-3 Rattan Jyoti, 18 Rajendra Place
New Delhi-110008 (INDIA)
Tel. : 25750801, 25820556
Fax : 91-11-25764396
E-mail : goodwillpub@vsnl.net
website : www.goodwillpublishinghouse.com

Printed at :-
Kumar Offset Printers
New Delhi

INTRODUCTION

Physiognomy, the science of FACE READING which means judging a person's face to tell his nature, helps one understand and analyse a person. Face reading, the Chinese art of predicting a person's fortunes by analysing the different elements of his or her face is over 2500 years old and was documented as long ago as the time of Confucius. The reader by looking at a person's face and studying the facial features gets sufficient information about his character, the potential, disposition, creativity and his good or bad fortune. It is a means to deeper communication with every person we meet.

The art of face reading has been in existence for thousands of years. In ancient Greece, Aristotle wrote expansively on physiognomy and his findings. Classical scholars such as Hippocrates wrote of face reading as a method of philosophy. In the Middle Ages, face reading was combined with astrology to become an integral part of the divination arts. By the 19th century, it was used as a method to identify potential criminals. In China, the art of face reading has always been considered as an indispensable tool to understand the human psyche and the fates.

Once one is able to learn what one is looking for, one can easily identify each feature that has shapes and sizes. Once the shape of a feature is determined, there is a definition of a personality trait associated with it. Each feature on the face, the eyes, eyebrows, nose, mouth and ears reveals something about a person's personality and the total picture is also affected by the overall shape of the face, forehead, jaw and chin.

Contents

CHAPTER 1

History Of Face Reading Or Physiognomy

The science of Face Reading is called Physiognomy. It helps you understand and analyse a person. You can make out by reading the face of person whether he or she is reliable or unreliable, honest or dishonest, cunning or simple, timid or dominating, practical or imaginative.

You can improve your relationship by knowing the nature of the person. You can understand their positive points and cope with their negative qualities.

By practice of observing the face of a person, you can judge him or her. Though all features speak a lot about a person, the entire character of a man should not be judged on the basis of one feature only. Various features represent various characteristics.

Face reading is a composite science. Faces need to be analyzed and read completely. Coming to conclusion, hastily should be avoided. A detail analysis should be done in order to judge person's nature by reading his or her face.

Physiognomy was prevalent in ancient and medieval times as well. During that period, there was lot of literature available for it. There is evidence in the earliest classical

literature that physiognomy formed part of the most ancient practical philosophy.

The earliest-known methodical essay on physiognomy is attributed to Aristotle. He examined the characters derived from the different features, and from colour, hair, body, limbs and voice.

The earliest theories were quite descriptive while the later medieval studies particularly developed the predictive and astrological side to their theories.

Physiognomy sometimes is associated with astrology because face reading also helps in foretelling. Physiognomy, which claims to find correspondences between bodily features and psychological characteristics, often makes use of supposed similarities.

In the 18th and 19th centuries, some people as a method of detecting criminal tendencies used physiognomy and still it is used for the same purpose.

In the 1920s, a judge of a US Superior Court, fascinated by the similarity between people he met in thousands of courtroom encounters, began a study of physiognomic (facial) traits. He tried to resolve the conflicting ideas prevalent. Through repeated observations, he arrived at sixty-four physical traits that he recognised as accurate indicators of character.

Also during the 1930s, personality studies began to consider the broader social context in which a person lived and cultural pressures in personality characteristics. For example, it has been shown that masculinity is not necessarily expressed through aggressiveness and that femininity is not necessarily expressed through passivity and acceptance. Physiognomy is now regarded as overly simplistic because most personality characteristics are manifested at different times in response to different situations.

In the 1960s, an American psychologist got his start in the face-reading business and he discovered that the face is such an extraordinarily efficient instrument of communication that there must be rules that govern the way we interpret facial expressions. He had established that expressions were the universal products of evolution. There were fundamental lessons to be learned from the face, if you knew where to look.

In order to become a good "face reader" you had to know a lot. Not only the knowledge accumulated for centuries, but also the psychology and diversity of facial traits determined by nationality and character. Today, physiognomy is widely used and it is being studied in the best-known colleges and universities. Participants will learn to identify and analyze the features of the face and gestures that characterise personality traits. There is a wide selection of literature describing physiognomy.

Suppose that you met a stranger. What is his personality like? What kind of job is best suited for him/her? What can we find out just looking at his or her face?

In many fields of work that require attentiveness and responsibility, a professional is not limited to perform his or her job based on the specific qualifications, but must possess the ability to 'read' faces. These professions include doctors, lawyers and psychologists.

Most people form their first impression of someone based on their intuition, even when not familiar with the concept of physiognomy. Similar examples we can find in the familiar phrases such as: *"silly face, keen eyes."*

However, our intuition is sometimes not enough to determine someone's character. The history provides a great amount of empirical evidence that correlates facial traits and indicators of character. There must be rules that govern the way we interpret physiognomic traits. Let's try to formulate the knowledge collected through centuries by the history of physiognomy.

The main conclusion that we can make from the history of physiognomy is that there is a great amount of experimental evidence that correlates facial features and character traits.

It is important to notice that charlatans and wisemen determined the rules of physiognomy. Their life and well-being depended on the 'accuracy' of their predictions. But how was the 'accuracy' of such judgment tested? It is doubtful that people used endless psychological tests in order to find an appropriate correlation. It is more likely

that the individual simply compared the diagnosis of the physiognomies with the opinion of friends and family.

CHAPTER 2

Face Reading Myths And Benefits

Physiognomy means judging a person's face to tell his nature. Face reading has been practiced for more than five thousand years. Face reading is different from reading expressions.

Probably reading expressions is very interesting but it has certain limitations. Deception is one. Since childhood, all of us have learned how to give a desired impression. Physiognomy shows things about faces that can't be faked or manipulated. Expression shows mood, which is a passing thing. Afterwards, reality sets in.

How Accurate is Face reading?

Since preachers began to teach Face Reading Secrets, they had read thousands of faces. At the end of each reading, feedback was asked about accuracy. About 99% of the time the response is positive. And this system is so easy to learn, students have a high level of accuracy, too.

Benefits of face reading

If you are a people watcher, you will find the inner behavior fascinating. Regarding practical benefits, they include better communication, personal empowerment, and

improved ability to see individuals rather than stereotypes.

Heredity and Face Reading

Genetics is part of the truth about life. It's not the entire truth. It may not even be particularly useful kind of truth in the context of face parts.

Truth has many levels, you know. After all, a cell from your hand, when seen under a microscope, seems entirely different from the hand you hold out to greet a friend. Yet both these perspectives of your hand are true. One of our privileges as human beings is the freedom to put our attention, at any one time, on whichever level of life we choose. We can make a mountain out of a molehill or a molehill out of a mountain.

Face reading is not perpetuating racism

Face Reading Secrets is not a pretext for judging people as good or bad. It is an opportunity to learn, not judge. Face reading secrets is not deterministic, because your face changes during your lifetime, and your face comes to reflect these changes.

Also face reading secrets is not about putting people into racial categories. It's about the shapes and angles and proportions within a face. It is not about color or texture of hair, color of eyes, or color of skin.

Face reading and Ethnicity

Stereotyping does set us up to expect certain features to go with particular groups. But when you look, really look,

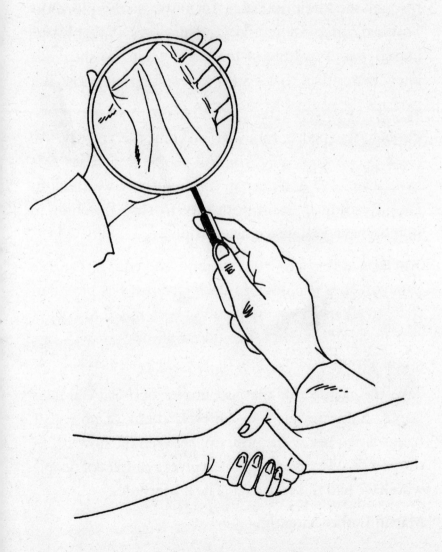

you see individuals. That's the fascinating part.

Once, an expert was interviewed on national television, the host asked this question: "How can you read faces of black people when they all look alike?" Shock waves ran through the studio audience. Interestingly, this talk show host had coffee-colored skin and blue eyes. Probably she, herself, was a mixture of black and white. So she really knew better than to ask such an insulting question. But perhaps she wanted to stir things up.

Publicly, few people today would come out and say, "All black people look alike" or "All people from East Asia look alike." We don't say it, but frequently we think it. Face Reading is an opportunity to stop thinking in stereotypes and start seeing individuals.

You look at one face part at a time, and within that face part you keep on looking. Each face part has plenty of traits to choose from. So if you've been raised to believe that certain face parts, like noses, always go with one ethnic group, you're going to be in for a big shock.

Take the example of the nose trait expert call the nose bonus. Some people have an extra chunk of nose that hangs down below the nose tip, between the nostrils. In the power of face reading, expert gives examples of people who have had this face data. The list includes:

Martin Luther King, Jr.

Albert Schweitzer

Anwar Sadat

Leo Esaki

Henri Bergson

Jacinto Benavente Martinez

Odysseus Elytis

Yuan T. Lee

Har Gobind Khorana

Camillo Golgi

Ivan Pavolv

Tiger Woods

With face reading secrets, a side benefit is that you discover new things about your own face you never noticed before, like ear position etc. Since 1986, experts have done thousands of Face Readings for people like you. And most have made surprising discoveries about their physical faces. How could this be? Before they did not pay close attention. .Why should they? Most face parts weren't meaningful. In fact, faces have so much information that a full face reading for one person can take an hour or longer.

Think of face reading knowledge like a TV set. When you choose to know more about people, zap! You can turn it on. When you are more interested in something else, say sex, your brain can be otherwise occupied. Automatically the part of you that does face reading will turn off.

The perfect Face

The perfect face does not exist. However, the Buddha's face is the closest to what we would term perfect. His face is completely balanced from the top, middle, bottom and side-to-side. His rounded chin and nicely shaped eyebrows create a sense of harmony and peace. And his very large earlobes suggest a great sense of wisdom.

In Chinese medicine, a beautiful face is a harmonious face. Grace Kelly, Catherine Zeta Jones and Jennifer Lopez all have incredible symmetry in their faces.

CHAPTER 3

The Five Elements Of The Face

It is important to note that most people are a mixture of elements with one prominent element.

The Wood element

Celebrity Wood faces include David Beckham, Kate Winslet and Tony Blair.

Wood encompasses growth, learning, new ideas, changing and moving. They are business people (often in Government) and in terms of health, wood is related to the liver and gallbladder. The Wood face is long and they are generally tall with a good physique.

Wood people are sensitive, indecisive and can often drink and eat too much rich food. They often harbour anger through frustration. An example of this was when David Beckham kicked a member of the Argentina team on the pitch during the World Cup in 1998.

They like to control and this can be seen in the power Tony Blair likes to possess.

The Earth element

Celebrity Earth faces includes Gwyneth Paltrow, Judy Dench, David Coulthard and Minnie Driver.

Those who possess an Earthy face are grounded, practical, energetic, enjoy dealing with materials, and are good with money. They are traditional types and take things slowly in a methodical way. Their physical appearance is robust and in health terms, the Earth element governs the digestive element.

The Metal element

Celebrity Metal faces include Victoria Beckham, Madonna and Shania Twain.

They are happy being in structure, very independent, excel in legal affairs and are media savvy. A prime example of this is Victoria Beckham and Madonna who are both always ahead with the latest trends and know exactly how to manipulate the media. They are also good counsellors.

A match of Wood and Metal together in the Celebrity world is David and Victoria Beckham. Metal tends to organise the Wood element and this is exactly how the press perceives their relationship - she wears the trousers. Victoria Beckham has a typical Metal face. She has naturally pale skin, larger cheekbones and a triangular face.

The Metal element governs the mind, lungs and colon. They also have a strong constitution.

The Water element

Celebrity Water faces include Russell Grant, Vanessa Mae, John Prescott and Queen Victoria.

The Water face is a rare one. Water personalities can be recognised by their round, chubby, soft faces. Large soft

eyes are a water feature as is dark hair and colouring. Water people are quiet, gentle and sensitive. They are good communicators and are sensitive.

They can be psychic and make good listeners, career counsellors. If the water is clear, they have strong reserves and the ability to flow freely in any situation. If it gets stagnant through unexpressed emotions, the skin can develop a blue tinge with dark rings under the eyes.

CHAPTER 4

Types Of Faces

Commanding Face

A commanding face usually has a round, dome-like head that signifies vast experiences in life. Dark, dense and slightly uplifted eyebrows reveal inner energy and vitality. People with such a face do not hesitate to take decisions, even in most difficult situations. Eyes are deep, penetrating and slightly closed at the outer corners. These indicate that the person has tremendous sense of superiority and self-confidence. These people do not give much importance to other people.

A long, straight and firm nose is a symbol of power. It speaks of great administrative and commanding qualities in the person.

Tightly closed lips with downward bend towards outer ends show a secretive nature.

How to recognise a commanding face:

1. Prominent nose

2. Cold and demanding eyes

3. Crooked and nasty lips

4. Long ears

5. Remarkable chin and jaws

Regal Face:

This is usually a beautiful face. Soft, dense hair shows an intense artistic nature. Full and charming cheeks bring out royal heritage. A large forehead indicates high intelligence. Eyes express inner vitality and strength. They have a magnetic quality that helps them draw attention. A nose with a ridge at the middle and perfectly proportioned broad nostrils again speaks of a commanding capacity but at the same time this power is mixed with charm and sympathy. Perfect teeth show good health and expressive nature.

How to recognize a royal face:

1. The face is not only beautiful, but also speaks of authority

2. Features like nose, lips and eyes are well formed

3. Temples and cheeks are full and charming

4. The chin is distinguishable

5. The ears are nice and appealing

Intellectual Face

Broad and high forehead signifies intellectual capabilities. Eyes are observing and philosophical. An outstanding nose is an indication of organizing and administrative capacity. Such a person commands respect of his or her friends and colleagues. The upper lip sitting well on the lower lip shows that the person is sensitive, talks less and works hard. Outsized ears indicate that the person is independent and thinks with his own mind.

How to recognize an intellectual Face:

1. Intellectual faces have some extraordinary features, like long nose, outsized ears, wide forehead etc.

2. Deep or philosophical eyes

3. The lips are pressed or otherwise, but definitely possess expressive quality

4. There is a humorous streak on such a face signifying independence and self-confidence

Diplomatic Face

A wide forehead speaks of a person's great experience with life and people. Eyebrows that are set part signal observation powers and understanding of human nature. The eyes are not only full of vitality and humor, they are also compassionate, understanding and deeply penetrating. A well-formed nose is an indication of a commanding, but not a bossy nature. Small, open and upward bent lips indicate that the person speaks a lot. He can express himself well and convince the listener.

How to recognise a diplomatic face:

1. Intelligent and expressive eyes

2. Wide and sloping forehead

3. Ears are big and well placed but they don't stand out

4. Cheeks are either full, or lean and furrowed

5. Lips should give an air of decisiveness

Simple Face:

A high and broad forehead is a sign of deep and broad intellect. Eyes show simplicity, straight forwardness and dynamism. Occasionally, eyes have a desire to do something useful. The nose indicates ability to lead and organise whereas the mouth signifies a firm nature. In short such a face looks well suited for all sections of society.

How to recognize a simple face:

1. Flat forehead

2. Normal hair - neither coarse nor thin

3. Open eyes, without any element of mystery

4. Lips are neither small nor wide or pressed

5. Normal nose

CHAPTER 5

Shapes Of Faces And Associated Traits

There are four basic face shapes, each with having own distinct characteristics. Very few people fall into pure type categories, but more often than not, the predominant shape will be recognisable.

The oblong type face

The Earth Type is considered as part and parcel of the other three categories in the Ayurvedic discipline. You will recognise yourself as belonging to this category by the longer, more oblong shaped face. You will also find yourself taller and possibly bonier than your squatter.

As an earth type, you are practical, methodical and deliberate but may tend to overwork. You will probably find the lion's share of workaholics in this category. You can be excessively concerned about material and financial security, so you push yourself to the limits in trying to acquire those things that remove this sense of worldly inadequacy.

In the process of your striving for success, you are severe

on yourself and others. Hopefully you are not of the lower type which is quite the opposite - tending to gross sensuality and emotional and dietary excess.

Some areas of physical weakness which may need to be watched include the skeletal and subcutaneous regions as well as your teeth and hair. The Earth Signs are Taurus, Virgo and Capricorn. As Taurus reflects the earthy sign, it regulates the throat and neck region so the thyroid and also lymphatic system is a constitution flashpoint.

Often the Virgo (another earth sign) suffers a nervous condition affecting the digestion. Vedic astrologers consider the sign of Virgo as the most sensitive in the Zodiac. The leaner Virgo, especially those given to the 100 hours workweek, must learn to be less fastidious and worried about results and simply relax and sleep a little more.

Modern western society, in particular, has glorified the earthy physique. The best looking actors and models, both male and female, tend to reflect the ideal mesomorphic shape. The danger of beauty lay in egotism, which in the lower examples of Mesomorphy is quite pronounced. This gives rise to numerous psychological issues creating obstacles in the area of relationships.

The Round Face

Round - Emotional

You can easily recognise a watery, emotional human being as the short and stocky type. If your facial shape and body structure is distinctly rounded and tending to a somewhat fleshy look, you'll fall into this category. Another designation for you is an endomorph.

Your body type means that you are predominantly emotional, sensitive and caring. Cancer is the cardinal water sign of the zodiac and symbolises motherhood and nurturing. This makes you extremely considerate and compassionate. You like to extend this facet of your nature into every area of activity, including your work.

You do however seem to have a natural tendency to interact with others, form an emotional base, making you mother to your peers.

And that is also the case if you are a male. You may take intense interest in your projects, desiring to nourish concepts from an inceptive stage, watering the idea at each and every step - much like a mother feeding her newborn infant. And just as a mother fearing the flight of her teenagers, at some point you also may have some lessons to learn about delegating tasks and letting go.

You are generally a conservative who is best suited to social situations and perform very well in professional arenas where a social and playful environment accommodates your naturally easygoing style. You also need and desire security and stability very much. You therefore have a natural affinity with money and finance and can do well in the home sciences, sales careers and the socially interactive professions like catering and hospitality. The banking and real estate sectors would also be ideal for your innate talents.

You may be prone to weight disorders and emotional difficulties, if you slot into this category at the other end of the scale. It means that emotions are perhaps not dealt with or digested correctly in your experience. This indigestion has its counterpart in the alimentary tract of your body. It is no coincidence that the medical fraternity refers to your type as an alimentive class of being. You do love food.

You also tend to retain excess fluid in the body, have a large chest, large magnetic eyes and thick hair. With Endomorphs, the Moon or Jupiter is usually prominent at the time of birth and so, according to astrologers and other alternative practitioners weight problems may become an issue for you.

The Water Signs are Cancer, Pisces and Scorpio. According to Hindu Ayurveda, the ruling water planets are Venus, Moon and Jupiter and hence Taurus, Libra and Sagittarius may be taken as water signs as well.

The Chinese face readers agree that you are a liquid and adaptable, sensitive and pliable individual. With other positive features, this is a good basis for success in midlife. It is more so if your neck is thick. The reverse holds true for thinner necked water types.

The Chinese readers also believe that being a full-faced endomorph means that you may feel family life imposes upon you and that your time is never fully capable of

being devoted to your other social passions. Compromise
will mark the evolved types while the less developed

amongst your class will struggle and perhaps fail at reaching the golden mean, as Buddha called it.

Strong sexual fantasies also feature strongly for you. Coupled with your natural charm and demonstrative affection, you can provide very loving and satisfactory romantic alliances, which last. Men of your nature prefer to stay in committed partnerships and function at their best when love and home are stable.

The Square Face

Square - physical

Well-built, muscular and energetic people are called Mesomorphs. Your face and head have a squarish shape, even your ears. You have a solidly built frame, which indicates your ardent interest in physical activities, sports and outdoor movement in general.

As a fire type you are seen to be aggressive, ambitious and dominating. You may be irritable and quick to anger but usually cool off just as suddenly. The sheer force of your approach intimidates others but they will always know where you and they stand.

Your mind is sharp and analytical and so you make a good practical worker, scientist, engineer or mechanic. Agility is one of your strengths. Others at first may not notice but your mind likes to look beneath the surface of things. So you'd make good researchers as well.

In health, you are prone to skin disorders, rashes and muscular strains and tears as a result of overexertion. In

extreme cases, you may be accident-prone through your impulsive streak. Your eyes too may also cause you problems at times. Fortunately, being endowed with strength and vitality, you are also blessed with strong recuperative powers.

You have an avid appetite and love eating but unlike the endomorphic water type, you tend to burn up calories rather quickly due to your continual activity. Furthermore, you have an excess of bile, which may create a need for a careful dietary program to assist your digestion because of over acidity.

The Fire Signs include Aries, Leo and Sagittarius. Scorpio can also be taken as fire as its sub-ruler is Mars.

The eastern characterologists consider the square a sign of stability and earthiness. No wonder you are regarded as an earthy. No nonsense type of individual who shoots from the hip. The 'Statesman's' face - e.g. Winston Churchill-possesses the square earthiness, which you share and portrayed his serious demeanor, deliberate and decisive decision making.

It's not usually evident but if you are a more refined type Mesomorph, you also have good communication and understanding with your romantic/marriage partners. You are able to reflect on problems and are capable of affectionately demonstrating your love.

The Triangular Face

Triangular - Mental

A rational temperament is known more technically as ectomorph nature. If you fall into this category of humans,

your head and face are easily recognised, as is your body type. You possess a slender wiry frame and your head is of an inverted triangular or pear shape. The high forehead indicates good intelligence, good high hairline, and unblemished good intelligence. You may make errors of judgement and choice in relationships and be suspicious, mistrusting and highly-strung.

Your veins are quite prominent with hair that is fine, soft or silky. Your type is usually very restless. You are one of those people always on the go - active, quick, versatile and talkative. Your voice may also seem somewhat high pitched.

Because the mental type is curious and investigative, all of the areas that allow free reign to your thirsty intellect will provide the best fulfilment for you. For the most part, you are known as an active, athletic and energetic individual but may somehow lack stamina and burn out quickly. You must learn the art of pacing yourself to maximise energy reserves.

Astrologically speaking, the air signs are Gemini, Libra and Aquarius. Even though Capricorn is an earth sign, astrologically it is assigned the property of air in Ayurveda. The planets ruling air are Mercury, Dragons Head and Saturn.

The Chinese face readers refer to your face as a Fire Face and this results in you being bright, intelligent, sensitive, creative and very active. These traits do reflect a fiery nature, and so coupled with your fine thinking capacity; you possess positive traits of both elements - fire and air.

Other popular types of faces

Broad Face

As the shape indicates, this one signifies a broad mind. One will also find qualities like tolerance and benevolence in broad-faced people. Such person looks at a broader picture and is not really bothered about intricate details. 'Forgive and forget' is generally their motto in life. These people are good administrators and executives, as steadiness and giving orders are their natural ways.

Thin and long Face

Inherent endurance and tenacity are characteristics of a long and thin face. If someone has a long face complemented by well-formed features, he or she is not the one who leaves things midway. Even when things go wrong they don't give up, for they seldom give up hope.

Pear-shaped Face

These people stand for sensitivity and intelligence. Depending on socio-economic conditions and educational background, these people can achieve great heights of creative and artistic brilliance. Most of the time, such people have interest in fine arts and they usually excel in these fields.

In introducing the general overview of the face, a couple more important points are noteworthy. They relate to the height and width of the head and face. A person with a developed back head is more emotional, family and socially orientated. The narrower the back head - the less so. The height of the crown indicates the idealism but more so the authority of the person. When the crown is low, the person lacks in confidence to the degree that the crown is underdeveloped.

Obviously, an overdeveloped crown produces a tyrannical, authoritarian nature. Next time you're in the office you'll be inspecting a few crowns on superiors heads. A well-developed crown also reveals an ambitious nature. The upper portion of the top of the head relates to imagination in proportion to its development and dominance.

Passivity can be detected by the width or narrowness of the head when viewed front on. The length of the head reveals foresight. A short head, when viewed side on indicates lack of forethought and a more live-in-the-moment attitude.

CHAPTER 6

The Hair And Forehead

The Hair

Your hair is a measure of physical insulation, endurance and overall strength. If your hair is fine, delicate and silky, you are sensitive and also likely to be fragile physically especially if you are of a slender build. Thick wiry hair is an indication of your physical prowess and your resilience in life. You have great restorative powers and may like a challenge in life.

The Forehead

The Forehead can be broadly categorised as follows -

A wide forehead expresses your cleverness and practicality - being someone capable of executing duty diligently. This gives you high idealism and a wealth of ideas. A high rounded and deep forehead depicts your idealism, but with a focus on strong friendship.

A narrow forehead is considered an obstacle to fulfilment, especially in social situations. Constraints in family life. Need to think things through.

Shallow forehead with a low hairline may cause many

obstacles to your career success and parental troubles between the ages of 15 and 30.

Flat forehead gives you a more pragmatic nature, given to factual expression.

Exaggerated forehead reveals you are certainly a dreamer - one who needs to anchor your ideas firmly to a plan of achievement.

The receding or flying forehead betrays your impatient and spontaneous manner in life.

Possessing an *indented forehead* is not a good omen for your employment or business prospects. Plan and work carefully. Indented with powerful eyebrow ridge means you are quick tempered, impulsive and ambitious.

A *pointed forehead* shows your high intelligence, if your hairline is set back and not too narrow.

CHAPTER 7

The Eyes

Most importantly, look to the eyes. *Prominent eyes* with bright sparkle or glitter are preferable to small, suspicious eyes, which reveal an introverted and secretive nature. In fact the eyes are the most important feature in your close encounters of the business kind. In your search for that employee or partner, look for eyes that sit firmly whilst gazing steadily. This reflects a solid and persevering nature and a person of stability and forthright disposition. In contrast, *a wandering eye* portends a nature given to unsettled and inconsistent habits. Restlessness will be evident and other features supporting your observation and gut feeling, a tendency to dishonesty and unreliability will be marked in this type. In short, this is a person of meager commitment.

Unevenly set eyes convey a unique meaning. Firstly, the person is capable of seeing things from a different perspective and applying lateral thought processes to resolving problems. These people will analyse your comments and observations with a left-of-field mentality. Often you will be amazed at the spontaneous insights that they offer. If you are looking for someone with a flair for shifting paradigms - then here is your man or woman. These people become invaluable assets to a company looking for ingenuity in its approach.

If the *eyes slant upwards* the person is an opportunist - more so if the brows also slant in that direction. Many models like Elle McPherson and Claudia Schiffer possess these eyes. They know how to get what they want. If the *eyes* are of the *opposite slant* i.e. *slanting downwards*, the person may be a little self-deprecating and at the mercy of others. They are hardly able to say no.

The late Princess Dianna and Michael Jackson share a feature of the eyes. They possess floating irises also known as sampaku. The whites are visible under the iris. This indicates an inner turbulence - a person at odds with the world. Though spiritual in nature, they are hard to please or understand and have very high expectations of others. Martin Luther King and Abraham Lincoln also shared these traits.

The whites visible above the irises may indicate some dangerous elements within the personality. An explosive temper may be latent in this type and the nature very forceful. Caution is the operative word in this case. Charles Manson exhibited these eyes. Chinese face readers call them wolves eyes.

Look at how close or widest the eyes are. Ideally, there should be at least one eye width between both eyes. That being the case, you can assume your subject has a balanced judgement and clear view of the world. The closer set the eyes, the narrower the opinion and view of the world at large. It may also reflect an over dependence on parental and family structures. These people may need a push to develop their own independent lifestyles. Their willpower should be strengthened in the search for their own self-assurance. Employees and workers displaying eyes of this type certainly need continual encouragement to grow in self-confidence. You will find these types possess little forbearance or tolerance and may crack under stress. Trivial matters can be blown out of proportion.

In contrast, the widest-eyed character is far more tolerant and broadminded in perspective. People of this class may present a flagrant disregard for authority and advice. A delicate blend of firmness and understanding will iron out the initial stresses between you and this type. Offer them alternative choices in their decision-making processes. In respect of career, these types need room to breathe. Give them plenty of space to explore their creative potential. At times, these types possess too broad and superficial an opinion.

Deepest eyes promise an intense, possessive, yet observant nature. When you look into the deepest-eyed person you can be sure that the mind motivating them is idealistic and inspirational. Often writers and creatively driven personalities possess deepest eyes. They are romantic to the core. Omar Shariff's or Val Kilmer's eyes represent this class. This idealism is tempered after the age of 35 and surprisingly, reveals a more than capable ability in financial matters. They are of sound judgement, compassionate and serious minded. A philosopher's face

may often also display a deepest soul window. You will need to carefully analyse and balance the other facial features to see whether this type is scattered and impractical. The square or round chin will anchor this type to a more empirical lifestyle. In this case, from a commercial point of view, the middle aged with deepest eyes may be a positive asset to you.

Besides, a *roving and unsteady eye*, one incapable of looking at you directly, is an attempt to mask inner intentions. Sometimes though, the shy and discouraged will also reflect a similar eye. The look in these cases is an important factor in discriminating between one and the other. Through practice the look can be ascertained quite easily and can reveal amazingly accurate character snapshots of your subjects.

What does the look demand? Some looks are cold, others attractive, angry, weak or strong. It is the look, which can override an otherwise attractive face. Soft, enticing features will be neutralised by a stern and unfeeling eye or a look, which is hard and cruel. Always balance your judgment of character by the look in the eyes.

Be watchful of people who look drunk even when they haven't had a single beer. Their eyelids sit very heavily over the eyes. Remember, don't jump to conclusions in any of your assessments. For example, the heavy lidded one may have had little sleep the night before. A sleepy or drunken look is one that is seen in both men and women. It offers a preview of a personality given to strong sexual

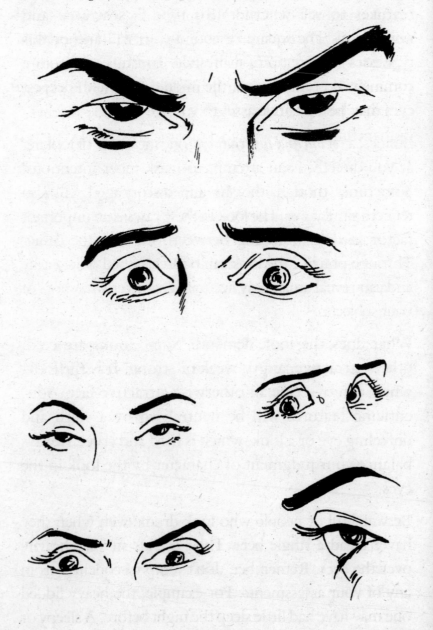

desire, more so if the lips are excessively thick and slightly opened. Periods of misfortune and depression are also revealed in this look. Cold and unflinching eyes with small pupils and sharp eye light may appear cruel. If the person possesses other features such as a pointed and downward turning nose, sharp angular shaped face and tightly pursed thin lips, be certain that the individual is indeed cruel - both mentally and even perhaps physically. This is a combo for ruthlessness.

The 'look' of the eye and its internal expression is something that cannot be taught in words but doesn't necessarily require years of experience to learn. In fact, we more or less instinctively do it when we meet people in various situations.

The colour of the iris is also an important determinant in your appraisal of character. A deep blue colour means that you are in the company of a highly sexed yet gentle and sensitive being. Light blue eyes suppose an individual who is likely to enjoy flirting with the opposite sex.

Deep green eyes are not only highly energised like their blue eyed cousins but very inventive too - both in practical and personal affairs. You will need a lot of time to understand the spontaneous and sometimes willful mind of a green-eyed person. Men and women of genius often possess this coloured eye. You'll need to sharpen your intellectual skills with green-eyed people.

Grey eyes reveal a high degree of intelligence and

imagination but passion may be less pronounced in this type as reasoning may subdue a part of their initiative. They are a refined class of people with a particular streak.

Black eyes are very rare and when encountered are extremely striking. They are somewhat strong natured individuals and don't always present their case with what you'd call, flair. You'd need to toughen up your skin to live or work with a black-eyed character.

CHAPTER 8

The Eye Brows

Bushy eyebrows:

Thick bushy eyebrows signify a forceful nature. Persons with such eyebrows are generally quite impressive. They are practical, realistic and independent. If the color of the eyebrows is darker than the hair on the head, it means that the person has strong feelings.

Light eyebrows:

Light-colored eyebrows, elevated over the eyes show lack of thinking power. Such people are usually quite carefree. If the color of the eyebrows is darker than the hair on the head it denotes bad health.

Widely set eyebrows:

Eyebrows set wide apart indicate broad-mindedness. These people neither suspect others nor criticize them. Usually, such a person would be friendly and easy-going.

Close-set eyebrows:

If a person's eyebrows are close and almost meeting, he will be critical and sharp eyed. He loves details and exactness. Such a person wants everything to be perfect according to his standards.

Tufted eyebrows:

These eyebrows are basically of masculine nature. They imply that the person easily loses his temper. These people are usually quite unstable, that is, they keep changing their opinions often.

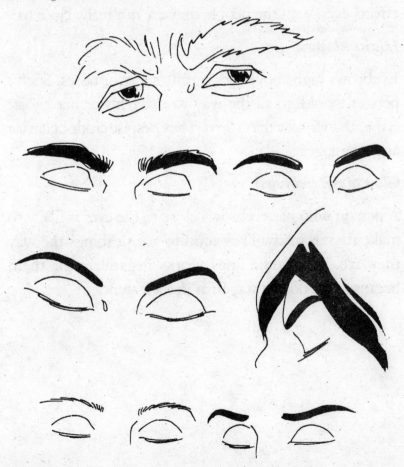

Meeting eyebrows:

If a person's eyebrows meet over his nose, jealousy comes naturally to him or her. Such a person would suspect others and would be obstinate and dictatorial.

Arched eyebrows:

Such people usually love dramatics. They love to surprise their friends. They love to create sudden and surprising effects even with the people they are not really close to.

High eyebrows:

Eyebrows high above eyes signify superior tastes. Such a person would go all the way to make his or her choice rather than follow the crowd. They despise crude behavior and language.

Close to eyes eyebrows:

A person who has eyebrows close to the eyes is likely to make friends easily. They tend to accept things the way they are. This sometimes works negatively for them because they do not stay firm in their stand.

CHAPTER 9

Lips

Normal lips:

These are of two types - vertical and with slight slant. Vertical ones characterize normal emotions and reactions, that is, nothing out of the ordinary. The lips with slant belong to people who are expressive and responsive. They are always ready to lend you a sympathetic ear.

Positive lips:

In this case, the upper lip is thinner than the lower lip and there is a clinching line between them. These belong to people with fixed aims and signify that they are already on their way to achieving them.

Good-natured lips:

These are also called female lips. The upper lip is plumpish and is well formed and the lower lip a little receding. Together these lips speak of a simple and likeable personality.

Experienced lips:

These have a downward bend, but this is not the bend of

despair. The slant indicates an ocean of worldly knowledge and vast experience. Too much has been known is the

message of these lips.

Professional lips:

These lips signify patience and efficiency. These are the lips of an experienced person and denote tolerance towards other people's ignorance and inefficiency.

Trusting lips:

When these lips open, you can see only the upper part of the teeth. Trusting lips are usually of equal thickness and moderate length. These lips characterize inner warmth.

Full lips:

Full and well-shaped lips not only enhance beauty, they also characterize generosity. Persons with such lips usually respond quickly and are kind. These lips speak of humanity and feeling.

Drooping lips:

These lips give out a signal of depression and doubt. But such persons are generally good sympathizers or benefactors.

Complacent lips:

These are the lips of achievers. These people give instructions, and hardly take them. These belong to people who move upward in life.

Extrovert lips:

Strong feelings characterize the people with extrovert lips.

These people are never ashamed of hiding their feelings.

Thoughtful lips:

The end of the lips taper into lines. They indicate that the person is more into his or her own world. These people usually don't take much note of what's happening around them.

Prominent lips:

Thick but well-formed lips speak of success and achievement. The equal thickness of the lips signifies a commanding nature.

Thin lips:

Pressed and thin lips show self-centeredness. These people usually can't see beyond their own interests. In some cases, pressed lips also signify lack of strength in one's character.

Smiling lips:

Besides smiles, these lips bring along a generous nature. These people are always ready to help others. These people seek fulfillment in helping others.

Noticeable lips:

The perfect shape of these lips always draws attention. These indicate that the person seeks perfection.

CHAPTER 10

The Nose

The nose makes a man! The nose holds significant importance in face reading. Short and fat or long and pointed, the nose shape not only defines one's personality but also tells a lot about his/her character.

Blunt nose:

A nose that is large and has a blunt tip signifies that the person is not formal with others. They are realistic people who have faith in themselves and are bold and harsh in their approach.

Small nose:

People with a small nose are said to be weak in character. They are people who are unstable in their decisions and lack reliability. They make commitments but are unable to fulfill it, as they are not serious in their behavior and approach.

Hooked nose:

A hooked nose indicates a person's passion to attain his or her goals. Such people are usually successful in their ventures.

Snub nose:

This type of nose indicates a person's insensitivity. It al
tells about the person's lack of maturity.

Aquiline nose:

An aquiline nose is straight and small. It is edgy from top to tip. Such people are selfish, emotional and have a wavering nature.

Perfect nose:

A nose of normal length and breadth, this is smooth, straight and unbroken. You can expect normal reactions from such people. People with perfect noses usually seek perfection.

Simple nose:

It is neither impressive nor attention seeking. As the name indicates, such a nose signifies a simple nature with not many outstanding qualities.

Womanly nose:

A small nose with a tilted tip is considered womanly in nature. These people are quite feminine in their behavior and approach. They lay a lot of emphasis on emotions.

Eagle nose:

Such people are rarely emotional. They have cruel tendencies and do not have a zest for life. They carry their ill feelings with them always.

Large nose:

Indicates initiative and drive. A well-shaped large nose signifies a strong character. Such a person would make his or her mark in a crowd. These people can put across their ideas clearly and concisely.

CHAPTER 11

Ears

Small ears:

People who have small ears are assumed to be hard working and goal oriented but the only shortcoming is that they lack confidence.

Pointed ears:

People with pointed earlobes are rigid and not easy going. They deviate from their stand only when there is no option left.

Round ears:

People with round ears are considered wealthy. Round ears signify love for material possessions.

Hairy ears:

Ears which have hair growing inside or around means that the person is laborious but he/she wastes energy on things which does not require much attention.

Wide ears:

Wide ears signify that the person strives hard to achieve

his/her aim and gains expertise in a particular field.

Flat ears:

People with flat ears are very attached to the family and are very caring in nature.

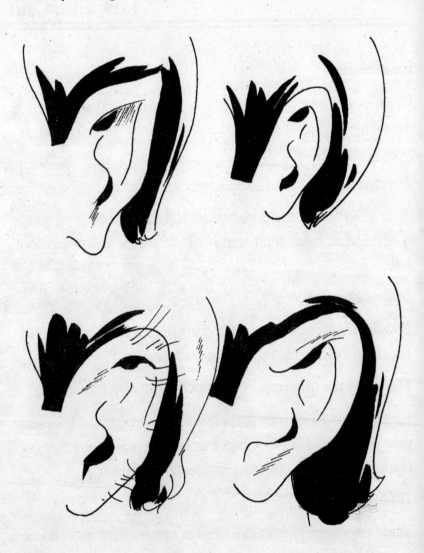

CHAPTER 12

Jaw and Chin

The chin and the jaw jointly form a unit. Their shape says a lot about a person's character. You can predict a simple thing, for instance, whether a person is stubborn or not by looking at his/her chin. This relates to the stamina of the individual and the stronger the jaw line, the greater the degree of stamina and endurance. People with very strong jaw lines can sometimes be considered stubborn. If the jaw line exceeds the balance of other features in the face, don't be too hasty in your judgement as this may simply mean a person who has strong convictions and who is not easily influenced by the opinions of others.

The chin should be **rounded or square** in shape with a gentle fullness. If this is the case, the latter part of life, during the 60's and 70's will be satisfying and lucky.

A **protruding chin** displays a strongly independent, determined individual.

Weak or receding chin reveals a weaker willed personality.

Jaw line extending beyond ear line betokens an individual who doesn't like losing and who may brook no opposition.

Protruding chin:

Jaw with protruding chin signifies that the person is imperative. In other words, the person does not entertain others' views and thinks his/her ideas are the best.

Square jaw:

Square-jawed people are determined and have the strength and capacity, to make their dreams come true.

Natural jaw:

People with a natural jaw are not the ones who would catch your attention. They are not of withdrawing nature. Such people handle normal day-to-day affairs but for complicated issues they need suggestions and assistance.

Balance jaw:

Such people do make their presence felt but not to a great extent. These are normal workers but if given ample opportunity they can achieve great heights.

Vanishing jaw:

Such features signify dependence on others. Such people never make an attempt to work on their own and become more like a parasite as they lack confidence and desire to do well in life.

Good jaw:

Such people do not have specific dreams to fulfill or goals to meet. They are very compromising in nature.

CHAPTER 13

The Cheeks

If status and position mean anything at all to you, you'll begin paying a lot more attention to the cheeks of your own and others' faces. Cheeks tell the story of

industriousness, power and authority in a person's life. Although westerners have a preference for a prominent and bonier style of cheek, the people from the east (especially Chinese face readers) have a different perception.

Ideally, your cheeks should be prominent, fleshy and high set with full body, colour and a warm glow. These attributes must be balanced against the position and strength of your nose. Both these features should harmonise with each other. The cheeks should stand somewhat apart from the nose not crowding it, nor too distant. The height of both should not detract from each other. If you do indeed possess fine cheeks of this description, you will have very good chances of all round happiness.

In describing the ideal cheeks, Santa Claus may spring to mind with his rosy and shiny set of chubby cheeks. But according to eastern opinion, the excessively shiny cheek is indicative of digestive trouble. The cheeks are a pretty good barometer of health changes from time to time. Keep a close watch on your own biological gauge, your cheeks. Other cheek colours to take note of in yourself and others are...

· *Overly red cheek*: lung and bronchial imbalance

· *Shiny and red:* gallbladder and/or heart problems

· *Red and rashy:* trouble in the intestinal region

And in the sphere of personal relationships, the colour of

the cheeks may also herald some very important changes. For example,

· *Blue or greenish tinge* - turbulence or difficulty in love life

· *Dark or grey tinge* - inner dissatisfaction and poor circumstances generally

· *Any moles* or marks, which appear suddenly, are indicators of danger or trouble through deception.

The stronger the cheeks, the more authoritative you are. Those in positions of control, executive power and leadership will often be seen to possess very strong, prominent cheeks. In romance and marriage, the partner with the more powerful cheeks is said to control the other. When meeting others of the opposite sex take note of the strength of the cheeks. Compare your own and study the play of energies between you. Who is the dominant partner? Do you or the other person own the stronger cheeks? In this way you should foster the spirit of understanding and insight into your relationships - both for business and pleasure.

If your cheeks are prominent yet not fleshy it shows your careful and economical disposition. You have a natural thrift not only where money matters are concerned but in virtually every department of life. You hate waste! You may be the one in the family who must eat the last vegetables left on your child's plate for fear that they may end up in the bin. Or, if you have a pet, you take pleasure

in seeing that no scraps have been discarded by being offered at the door of the kennel for the next morning's breakfast.

Undeveloped cheeks means you are not that forceful in your communication style and tend to be a little laid back but usually quite happy with what providence brings along. You must be a little wary that this doesn't deteriorate into an apathetic stance, which may cause lost opportunities for you.

Sometimes the cheeks appear to be strong in their presentation and are pronounced but lacking at the base. This means you are a forceful individual who is combative by nature. You are reactive to the circumstances and people around you and are learning the lessons of graciously living and letting live.

If your cheeks are narrow but strong you have a very stubborn streak in your nature. You are not easily changed in opinion or persuaded from the course of action you set your mind upon. You are also extremely forceful in the way you present your opinions and ideas to others. This may not serve you as well as you think - especially if you require the support of your peers and superiors in your professional arena.

The Philtrum

The groove on the upper lip, below the nose is worth mentioning. It is called the philtrum. If it is clearly marked,

deep and long, it foretells for a strong and healthy ener;
levels and vitality. Flat, weak and unpronounced philtrur
are a mark of reduced life force and drive.

CHAPTER 14

Face Reading The Chinese Perspective

Human beings possess three bodies. First, there is the physical body, which you can see and is tangible. It is solid and has a shape, a color and a texture. The second and third bodies are the mental and the spiritual, which are intangible and merge with the physical body. Our true nature begins to take on a physical form in our face. It is where our emotions and our state of health are first revealed. And, as Shakespeare pointed out in his play Mac Beth: "There's no art to find the mind's construction in the face." For the face is truly an opened book.

For thousands of years, the ancient wise people wondered if our facial features could determine our fate or personality. They began to compile individual studies, one feature at a time, to see if there was a direct correlation between facial features and specific fates. In ancient Greece, Aristotle wrote extensively on physiognomy categorizing his findings into six chapters that included physical characteristics of face, body and voice. The Classical scholars, such as Homer and Hippocrates, wrote of face reading as an ancient method of practical philosophy. In the Middle Ages, physiognomy was combined with astrology and became part of the divination arts. By the 18th and 19th century, it was used in Europe as a separate

study of criminology where facial features were used to identify potential criminals. In the 20th century, it was lost to folklore and superstition. But, face reading has reemerged in the 21st century as a guide in psychoanalysis or, as a tool for a competitive edge in the executive boardrooms of corporate America. It is no longer a parlor game. The continuous interest in face reading has given weight to an art that the Chinese have always known has been an important guide in human understanding.

In China, the father of face reading is often credited to the philosopher Gui-Gu Tze, who lived during the Warring State Period (481-221 BC). His book Xiang Bian Wei Mang is still in print to this very day and is studied by serious students of physiognomy.

The Chinese art of face reading is a very involved system that classifies facial features individually by judging the color, shape and disfigurements of specific areas of the face. Basically, the face is partitioned into 108 areas. Each area is a specific age and life situation and by observing the Five Elements of the productive/destructive cycle and the Taoist theories of yang and yin, it may be possible to predict events, diagnosis illnesses or to understand a person's personality.

We now measure the face into the Three Stages of the Chinese trinity of Heaven, Man and Earth. The First Stage, which is Heaven, starts at the hairline down to the eyebrows. This represents our childhood. The Second

Stage, which is traditionally known as Man, starts at the brow and ends at the area just below the nose tip. This is our middle years. From the nose tip to the bottom of the

chin is our old age or the Third Stage and it is called Earth. It is important that the distance between each Stage is even in length. If one Stage is less than 1/3 in size then life could be difficult at that particular period of life. A short, narrow forehead may indicate an unhappy childhood. A large forehead may tell us this person will come into society early. The Second Stage announces: "This is my life!" If it is open or has a happy feeling then this person may have, thus far, a good life. But, a short Third Stage may reveal a short life contrary to a long chin, which indicates a long life.

There are Four Turning Points of Life on the face. They are called Gates. The first Gate is between the eyebrows or the Third Eye and it is the age 41. The second Gate is located just under the tip of the nose and it is the age 51. The third Gate is right under the lower lip and it is the age 61. And, the last Gate is at the bottom of the chin and it is the age 71. These Gates are considered a 'critical age' and that any scars, lines, inauspicious moles or blemishes here may predict difficulties around that age.

The Chinese also use the shapes and characteristics of the Five Elements to further describe a personality. A Fire face will be pointy like a triangle. For example high, prominent cheekbones. They could be quick-tempered. A Wood face is long, rectangular in shape. They could be stubborn. A Water face is soft and round and may posses a long jaw line. They can be flexible. Whereas, an Earth face is thick and they may be generous. And, a Metal face is square, especially the jaw and forehead. They can be self-indulgent.

The ancient Chinese also made a distinction between what was considered fortunate or unfortunate for either a female or a male. In order to keep harmony in a marriage what may be desirable on a man was not desired on a woman. For example, high prominent cheekbones and a very high forehead on a woman would not make a desirable mate. That's because high cheekbones indicate aggression and competitiveness and a very high forehead is power. The ancient sages felt it was best that only the man wore the pants in a household. But, a look through any fashion magazine can tell you that in modern times high cheekbones are considered attractive, as well as, a prerequisite for any aspiring fashion model or actress. But, if you think about it you'd have to be aggressive and competitive in a profession like that.

In Chinese face reading, we also have The Twelve Houses. These are 12 points on the face representing various life situations from the First House of Fate, positioned between the eyebrows, to the Second House of Siblings (eyebrows) to the 4th House of Children (under the eyes) and so on.

The Chinese technique of face reading starts with the ears: the left ear tells your fate from birth until the age of seven, while the right ear corresponds to the ages of age 8 to 14. Next, the face is divided into 3 sections. The upper section includes the forehead, which determines your fate from age 15 to 30 and is called the celestial region. As the name suggests, your life during this period is dependent more on heaven than on your own efforts, and you are more or less protected by your parents and ancestors. The middle section, called the human region, runs from the eyebrows to the nose and dictates your destiny from 31 to 50. During this period, your success or your fortunes will rely mostly on your own efforts. Finally, the lower section, called the earthy region, includes the bottom of the nose to the chin and concerns your fate after the age of 50. This is a period in which your achievements on the earth are already well established.

If the three regions are equally proportioned, you will have a balanced life throughout your existence without any drastic changes, good or bad. If any of the three sections is larger or smaller than the other two, it means your fate will be better or worse during the corresponding time.

The eyebrows can reveal one's destiny at the start of the middle years. The space between them is particularly important. In general, long, thick eyebrows are considered good, and the wider the space between the eyebrows, the better.

The eyes reveal your intelligence and your attractiveness to other people. Large eyes are generally considered more favorable, according to the art of Chinese face reading. They are associated with intelligence, wisdom.

Your cheeks determine your fortune throughout your

forties. Generally speaking, well-developed cheeks are considered best. They show that you have plenty of energy and are usually self-confident.

The nose is linked to personal wealth. Thus, by studying someone's nose, you can tell whether that person will be financially well endowed or not. It is also believed that the key to divining a man's sexual power is his nose. A straight nose is linked with success in life.

The mouth belongs to the earthly region and determines your fate after the age of 50. This is a period during which your achievements on the earth are already well established. Your mouth can reveal a lot about your wealth during this period of time, as well as your sexuality (especially if you are a woman).

The chin also belongs to the earthly region and reflects your destiny beyond the age of 60. Generally speaking, a broad and rounded chin is most desirable, as it will bring prosperity to your old age.

Below is a brief summation of auspicious and inauspicious qualities of some facial features:

A summary of the ears:

Auspicious: Above the eyebrow level; long earlobes; flat against head; wide door.

Inauspicious: Small earlobes; leaning forward and narrow door.

A summary of the eyebrows:

Auspicious: Dark, thick, long; smooth and orderly, high above eyes.

Inauspicious: Sparse, thin, pale, short; chaotic; close to eyes.

A summary of the nose:

Auspicious: High, straight bridge; big, round tip, fu
fleshy wings; invisible nostrils.

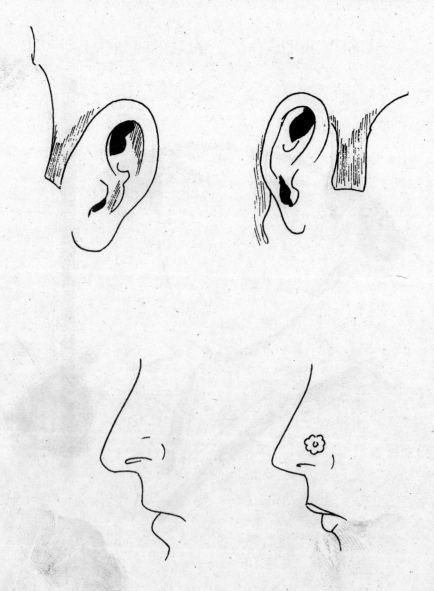

Inauspicious: Low, crooked, hooked or bumpy bridge, pointed or upturned tip; thin wings; visible nostrils.

A summary of the mouth:

AUSPICIOUS   INAUSPICIOUS

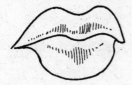   

AUSPICIOUS   INAUSPICIOUS

AUSPICIOUS   INAUSPICIOUS

Auspicious: Rosy colored, thick, broad squared shape, symmetrically balanced and lips closed.

Inauspicious: White, dark colored, thin, a small shape, symmetrically unbalanced, lips opened.

A summary of the chin:

Auspicious: Full, fleshy, broad and long.

Inauspicious: Thin, short, pointed or receded, dimpled or broken.

A summary of the eyes:

Auspicious: Large size, wide-set, dark pupils with silvery whites.

Inauspicious: Small, close-set, Small pupils and discolored whites.

CHAPTER 15

Celebrity Face Readings

Daniella Westbrook

Classic beauty is the first impression conveyed by Daniella Westbrook's enticing visage. Though not a specific feature, radiance and magnetic appeal are evident from her features and this one quality is obvious in those we consider beautiful. Daniella is, of course, no exception.

That she is an expert in bedroom arts can be seen in her hot eyes, full, seductive lips and soft skin. The developed jaw line indicate that she may also enjoy taking the lead and initiating her love 'craft' as a means of asserting herself with men. In romance however, over the long term, Daniella's thinner upper lip reveal a nature that can, at times, find it hard to give and yield, unless there's something in it for her.

Daniella's low set and sharp eyebrows transmit a distinct warning signal for us all: " I'm hot, I'm rash and ready to go!" She needs to act quickly on her instincts and intuitively knows when to move. At times, this comes across as an irritable and edgy side to her nature (as her closest friends and family members may attest). Still, this one trait coupled with the straight lip line point to a dedicated and hardworking, reliable individual who gets things done.

A certain self-indulgent tendency is seen in Daniella's nose

shape. The fact that she hasn't always made the best choices in friendship and love can be seen by the lack of scrutiny in her nose tip, which lacks body in the nostril region. Even as she enjoys a diverse social life, the slightly pronounced cheeks and jaw area also fuel her taste for excess in this area and hint at a love of the high life. An excessively developed jowl highlights a demanding and somewhat bossy nature. Daniella's chin adds fuel to these character traits by its prominence and foretells of her need to be right. Those with a pronounced chin do indeed lead with their chins and this is borne out in her case.

As a whole, her finely carved facial structure shows us her refined and artistic passion. This tells us that Daniella takes pride in her work, home and personal appearance and likes to express elegance through all her actions. Taken to the excess though, this could result in an extreme self-absorption and sense that she isn't as good as we all think. Her self-esteem may waver between self-love and self doubt and this challenge may continue until she discovers her true beauty as a caring, warm and sensitive being. This personality trait is also seen in the softness of her desire eyes.

By combining these facial traits above and also looking at her well-formed cheeks, we see that Daniella will aspire to artistic power. The cheeks signal the status and power we might expect to see in an individual. Along with strong sparkling eye glitter we can anticipate a successful attempt at acting, theatre and other expressive arts, which will provide Daniella the attention and fame she seeks.

Victoria Beckham

By studying her face, one easily recognises the fiery, creative and restless character of Victoria Beckham. With her slender thin frame, inverted triangular or pear shaped face - a high metabolic rate and cerebral approach to life are indicated. The high forehead always indicates intelligence but in Victoria's case may tend to drive her round and round in circles. She tends to rationalize her life away. She is no doubt a thinker, an 'ideas' person. The intensity and drawing power in her eyes disclose intelligence and a challenging prove-it-to-me attitude. Brown eyes are also passionate.

If it wasn't for her very strong and broad nose, Victoria's intense lifestyle could adversely affect her health as she can become highly-strung and reactive when she overloads her plate with too many deadlines. Her broad nose is also a dead giveaway for her love of friends and admirers. The other saving grace is her extremely broad and deep philtrum (groove above the lips). This gives her boundless physical energy with sexual curiosity and a clever lovemaking style. Though she will have ample lovers, the unique diamond shape to her face reveals a deeper fear of not finding her true soul mate in her life.

Her 'v' shaped eyebrows are precise and show determination, persistence and an ability to get things done. Because they are set low upon her eyes, there is an impulsive streak, which causes Victoria to implement her ideas quickly. Her neat ears support and balance this fact

and demonstrate she is tidy and careful in performing her
duties. As they have a 'roundish' shape, this declares her

taste for music and dance – which have made her famous the world over.

The sensual lips of Victoria also exhibit a slight downward turn at the edges. This is the mark of a demanding and verbal individual who has no hesitation in making her desires and her displeasure known very quickly. If Victoria can come to terms with the emotional side of her nature she will acquire spiritual fulfillment as well as continuing professional success.

Britney Spears

At the recent MTV awards, Britney Spears stunned the world with that now historic clincher with Madonna. Let's look at what some of her facial features reveal through face reading...

Britney continues to dazzle us with her powerfully captivating performances. She possesses those classic traits of beauty and luster, which exude from her face. Her eyes also radiate a bewitching, self-assurance. This is called glitter and is one of the facial indicators of her success and popularity.

Her shining, attractively dome-shaped forehead tell us she is idealistic. The forehead has three divisions – imagination, memory and observation. In Britney's, due to the dome shape, her imagination is most pronounced. These features tell us about her high intelligence and thirst for knowledge.

Her finely shaped nose is a sociable one. It is quite solid and indicates a need to be surrounded by admirers. Her

cheeks are full and rosy and these also add weight to the fact that she enjoys a fun time with friends. Because her nostrils are not too visible, it's a great sign of wealth and material fortune.

Her chin and jaw segments are in good ratio (in proportion) which means a persistent and energetic personality. Physical dexterity is a reflection of this feature. Britney goes the extra mile and is an atomic dynamo in performance as a result. Her twenties are a very successful time for her because the forehead relates to the years 18 to 30. Thereafter her eyebrows, from 30 to 34 rule her life and these are finely shaped as well.

A man will have to keep Britney ever on her toes as she demands high intelligence in her partners (high forehead and clear eyes). Her slightly elongated eyes show that she may quickly lose interest in the object of her attractions if not fulfilled readily.

Ben Affleck

The angular yet symmetrical face of Ben Affleck is a good reflection of hard work and luck combined.

The ridge above his eyes reveals a highly observant nature and even practical and dexterous thread to his character. This also means a good rise in fame and status after his 28th year.

Ben's eyebrows are humane and his lips tell of a somewhat reserved element, which may make it hard at times to guess what's going on in that brain of his. Whatever it is, the high forehead and neat, straight hairline are testimonies of highly refined intellectual skills and also perfectionism in work and personal areas.

The strong jaw, dimpled and somewhat prominent chin, however, point to a stubborn and aggressive streak to his personality.

Penelope Cruz

Beauty and power obviously radiate from Penelope Cruz's face. Face reading reveals a little more about her somewhat hidden character.

Penelope's bewitching gaze, large eyes and succulent lips reveal her expressiveness - the full eyelids representing an observant yet intuitive personality. Her slightly uneven lip setting and dimples at the edge portray a challenging conversational style. Her strong, wide cheekbones and diamond shaped face demonstrate a dominant expression in relationships.

Her lovers need special talents to satisfy her assorted romantic interests. But her dramatic eyebrows, promise further acting successes.

Russell Crowe

Besides his handsome good looks, there are other signs in Russell Crowe's face that could have predicted his success. As we divide his face into the Three Stages, we see his high broad forehead as an indication of a good childhood. His forehead is long and wide which indicates intelligence and a good imagination. A shiny forehead tells us he is destined for success and recognition. The eyebrows, which represent siblings, are straight and orderly and this says that his relationship with them is good. However, his brows are set quite close to his eyes, which reveal his impatience for others, even for the slightest offense.

The First Gate, the area between his brows, is auspiciously

wide but is marred by a mole. This could indicate some difficulties in life, especially around the age of 41. His attractively fleshy, plump nose tip gives him a warm and friendly spirit.

Russell's long chin means a good life in his old age, but

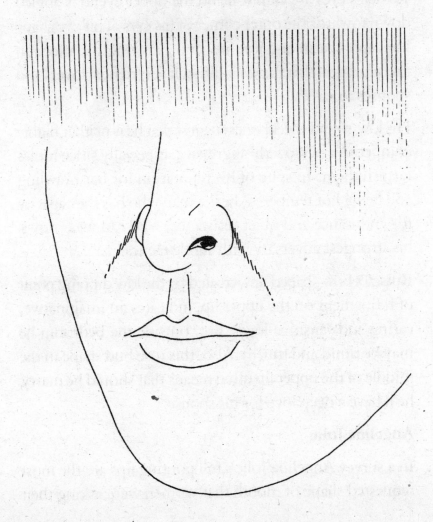

the slight dimple may indicate a strained close relationship later in life. His ears are close to his head and are positioned above his eyebrows. This is a favorable position for the ears, for he will be well respected and have a high social status early in his life.

Russell's eyes are elliptical and the upper eyelid is angled down towards the outer corner of his eyes. This eye shape indicates charm and jealousy and a craving for affection and attention that makes it difficult for friends, lovers and spouses to satisfy.

His low, round cheekbones suggest that he is neither highly competitive nor overly aggressive, especially since moles tarnish them. In spite of his reputation for bar brawling and being hot tempered, he is a man who has the capacity for endurance and quiet resistance, who can wear down his strongest adversary with subtle tactics.

Russell's bow shaped lips, created by the low dipping point of refinement on the upper lip, indicates an imaginative, caring and sensitive lover. But, outside the bedroom he may be timid and touchy. Also, this rose bud shape in the middle of the upper lip often means that should he marry, he'll have a deep love for his spouse.

Angelina Jolie

In a survey Angelina Jolie's full pouting lips are the most requested shape of mouth that women were asking their plastic surgeons to give them. And, no wonder, for thick lips were found to be honesty, loyalty and friendliness. People with thick lips enjoy delicious food, but may have poor taste in general. Other inauspicious qualities are, surrendering too much to their emotions and excessive sexual indulgences.

Angelina's mouth tells that she is very demanding of the affections from others. Her sexual appetite is also very strong. However, the top lip is shorter than the bottom, which says that she can reach sexual satisfaction before her partner. On the positive side, her lips indicate good health, intelligence, lasting friendships and a rewarding life in her old age.

Angelina's eyebrows are not asymmetrical. Since the eyebrows represent siblings it may mean she has stepsiblings (half brothers/sisters). Eyebrows that don't match often suggest one's parents are separated or there's a fluctuation in the family life. Personality-wise, it can also indicate moodiness. Her eyebrows are arched high above her eyes, which make her very tolerant of others, as well as, patient and easy going. She makes friends easily and keeps them forever.

And then there are those high cheekbones and large eyes, which from an Asian point of view indicate a strong desire to compete while large eyes make her extroverted and outspoken. A woman's nose is called the Husband's

Star. Her nose has a round nose tip and a straight bridge that

is not, too high, which traditionally secures a loving husband. Her visible nostrils say that she is a not good with money.

Face reading can be quite challenging and insightful. It can help you to better understand the people around you. First impressions will have new meaning to you when you find yourself accurately predicting personalities, future events or possible health problems.

John Kerry

John Kerry has a very thin, long face. This means he is a hard-worker and has a strong desire to reach the top. He will work more hours than there are in the day to obtain his goals. Success and his ego are extremely important to him and losing isn't an option to him. He will do whatever it takes to get what he wants.

He is very concerned with how things look. No matter what happens, he is skilled in putting a positive spin on it to make it look right to others. His focus is on his ambitions, ego and appearances. He is an expert storyteller and can be very believable because of his non-threatening style. His eyes show that he is very good at knowing what people think and because of this strength he has developed a finely tuned ability to confront and acknowledge their issues or objections, even before they have a chance to voice them.

He has incredible will power and it may appear to others

that he actually wills things to happen with his forcefulness. His eyebrows show that he is slow to get started on

projects, but once he does take one on, he can see it through all the way to the end. He is a logical, step-by-step thinker and solves problems in a sequential manner. He does not connect with people on an emotional level. He much prefers to hear the facts, rather than how it made them feel. Sometimes, he can appear very Spock-like to others.

His eyes show that he is skeptical. He doesn't believe what he is told and he is not trusting of strangers. This caution even carries over into his personal life, because he shows that he is also distrustful of people who are close to him. His eyes also show that he doesn't reveal very much about himself. He holds these things very close and does not open up about his true feelings often or easily. When speaking about situations or other people, he speaks freely. Not so, when it comes to what is on the inside and how he really feels. No one really knows the answer to that question, except for him.

He is very pessimistic and expects problems. When problems happen, they come as no surprise to him and he confronts them head on. He is usually prepared to conquer anything that comes his way, because he does his homework. He does not like surprises. When he is surprised, his chin shows that his first reaction is to lash out in defense. His eyes show that he would then regain his composure and deal with the surprise. It is this first reaction, however, that has saved him in the past, but could sink him in the future.

His eyes show that he has suffered in the past and connects with people on that level. He was born to be a doctor or psychologist. However, the physical, more masculine part of his personality demands that he be more active, so those fields of work involving healing would seem much too slow for him.

His nose shows that he must be in control in his work life. He wants to control everything from the surroundings, to the pace, to the style. He will even tell others around him how to behave, to fit with how he thinks it ought to be done. He will listen to the advice of men over women and had a strong male influence in his life.

His eyelids show that he must have his own space and doesn't like to be boxed in – both in his personal relationships and on the job. He may be overly critical of others. He sees dependence as a sign of weakness and doesn't tolerate it.

His ears show that he is very good at knowing what other people think. He has spent his life fine-tuning this ability and can anticipate problems before they happen. He does have strength as a psychologist and in healing sicknesses of the mind because he can spot them so easily. He is also good at spotting psychological weaknesses and will not hesitate to take advantage of those in his enemies.

His mouth is small, but he has the chat lines. He is accustomed to winning arguments. He will back down

when the conversation turns personal, as he doesn't like
to talk about that area. He also needs to be in control of

the conversation and if challenged to the point that the control goes to someone else, his desire to lead may cause his mouth to open before he is ready. He has developed much more self-control than he has had in the past, but the trait is still there.

The shape of his face indicates that he is very aggressive in carrying out his actions. This means that he will try hard to get his way. He works very hard to hold onto his power at all cost. His whole identity is rooted in how much power he has at the time. When the power goes away, so does he. He is what he controls.

His eyes disclose that he doesn't reveal much, if anything, on his business side. He is extremely mistrusting of others and tends to trust in his own gut feelings. He is an island and alone, even within his own circle. He never really feels included or a part of, and most of that comes from the environment he creates. In all of his photos, his right eye was always visibly smaller than the left eye, although both eyes are very small. Small eyes mean he is focused and has a definite aim. He is very secretive. He holds information back and releases it only when it would have the greatest impact. He prides himself on his ability to get the goods on other people, whether it is through his own investigative work or through outside sources. He has a tremendous investigative tendency. Had he not chosen politics as a career, he would be suited for a career in detective work.

However, keeping secrets has also hurt him – which is why his right eye is smaller than his left eye. He has

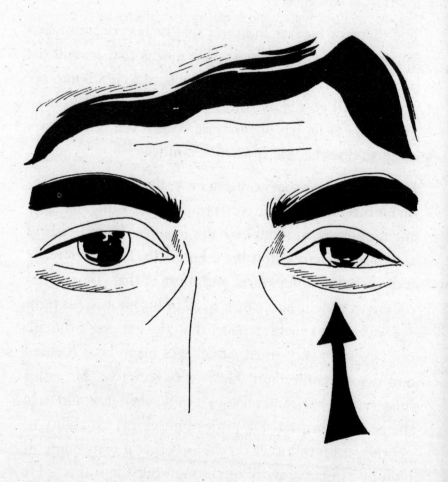

become distrustful to the point that it caused physical problems in this photo. He also needs to watch his blood pressure. He is critical of others and impatient and these traits are causing unnecessary stress.

The focus lines in between the eyebrows are very visible, even when his face is relaxed. This means that he goes all out for what he believes, and will do just about anything to accomplish his goals. Sometimes, this extreme focus causes him to miss the bigger picture. Seeing the bigger picture hasn't always been easy for him. When he does grasp it, he is usually quite realistic and balanced in his viewpoints and action. When he is focused on getting his way, he is very biased. Challenging him, when he is in this mode does no good, he will be too defensive. However, when confronted with facts, lots of facts, he will usually back down as he starts to develop the bigger picture.

His nose indicates that he does what he does because he wants to, not for the money. He grew up feeling quite insecure. This insecurity has carried over into his adult years and is what continues to give him the feeling of always being 'alone'. He always wanted more as a child. He wanted more of everything and it wasn't there, so he withdrew. One of the ways to kill the dragon of isolation was to go into public life. That was a huge step for him.

His nose also shows that he is spontaneous and lives in the moment. This is another reason he is not very good at seeing the bigger picture. He may have grown out of it, but in his earlier years, his motto was 'if it feels good do it.' He has a rebellious streak in him, which could cause

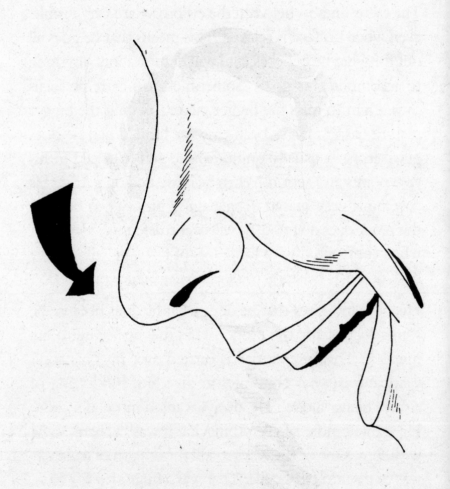

him to try risky behavior, even when getting caught could mean the end of everything. His chin shows that he has confidence he would never get caught.

His cheeks show that he has intense energy and works i
bursts. He could blast in like a tornado for a few hour:
then retreat. Those around him may think they are sittin
in the eye of the storm. He can get a lot done in a ver
short amount of time. He needs deadlines. Without
deadline, he may not start the project.

Dick Gephardt

His ears reveal that he marches to the beat of a differei
drummer. He does not follow the crowd or the norn
Although he has a good understanding of what most peop
want, he tends to want to act contrary. This may relate i
his inner power struggle. He is self-assured and gai
satisfaction from holding his ground when it goes again
the current.

His mouth again carries the theme of the eyes, in that l
is distrustful of others, especially if they bring good new
He tends to believe bad over good. He is hard to convinc
He is cunning and his words can be razor sharp. Agai
he is extremely secretive. He will tell you what he thin
you want to hear.

His eyebrows are hidden, which means he is a chameleo
He can get along in many different groups and situatio
and can adapt easily to the environment. In fact, he thriv
on changing environments. If he is in one place too lor
he gets anxious and must move. This could relate to l
desire for adventure, which is shown in his chin and l

nose. He is always on the move and it is a trait that
makes him difficult to work for, especially if he just assumes
that other people can keep up. His focus of thinking is on

being in control. He does not like to be told how to think. He will invite ideas, but will only consider those that come as suggestions. If he senses a demand, he will discard it. The best approach is to go head on with your idea, stand your ground and be prepared with facts. If he senses weakness, he will go directly to that weak point. This is where his words can be razor sharp. He will then use the secrets he has held for the kill.

His chin is large wide and strong. He is assertive and forceful. His chin is uneven, it goes up on the right side, which makes it smaller than the left. This means, that on his personal side, when he give his word, it is set in stone. On his business side, when he gives his word, it is not set in stone. The entire right side of his face is smaller than the left side. He relies on his personal life and extracurricular activities to energize him.

CHAPTER 16

Face Reading And Adoptions

Face reading and adoptions

Making the decision to adopt is a huge undertaking. The whole focus is to bring a child into your family to love as your own. Problem is, the child you adopt has a set of birth parents out there that are linked with the child from the moment of conception.

Much has been discussed about the role birth parents play in the lives of adopted children. Conventional wisdom has swung from once believing in complete denial of the birth family to open adoptions with even mandated visits with birth family. The prevailing mood of the times seems to dictate what is best in the best interest of the child.

With the discovery of DNA and genetics, science has established that children inherit their traits from their birth parents. While nurturing can have a tremendous influence on how traits manifest themselves ever time, the basic blueprint for who we are in the world comes on the day of conception.

Face reading meticulously examines the features of a

person's face and connects those physical characteristics with personality traits. Since adopted children do not inherit their genes from their legal parents, the chances that the

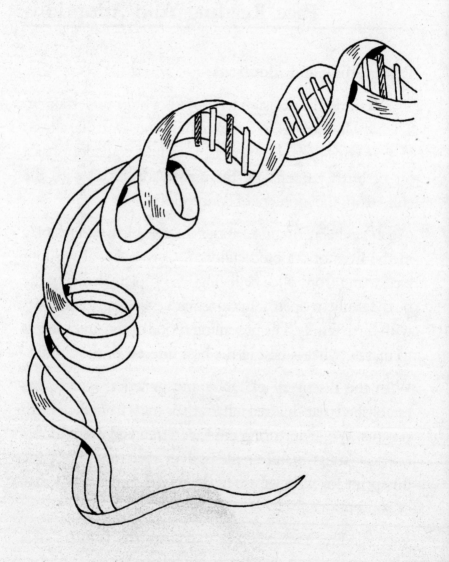

physical traits of these new parents are different from those of the birth parents are pretty high, especially if the child adopted is from a different ethnic or racial background.

Face Reading opens a window of discovery that allows the child and the parents to learn about the birth parents from a neutral place. There is no right or wrong way to have your eyes placed in your head; it is not better or worse to have a sloping forehead or a more squared forehead; there is no value judgement placed on the distance between your nose and your chin.

Taking measurements of the face of the child and the adoptive parents offers the chance to get to know and understand each other in a whole new light. The child experiences himself or herself as being seen and understood, and also feels a sense of relief in understanding his or her adoptive parents and how to best communicate and engage with each other. And everyone gets to feel a sense of connection, a sense of knowing, with the birth family.

A child can look at the high arching curve of his eyebrows and know that his birth mother or father was dramatic and loved to be on-stage.

A child can learn that her nose turning down means that her birth father or mother was rather skeptical.

Once the physical traits are linked with personality and birth parents, then what?

Your family is then armed with a powerful set of tools for encouraging innate strengths and redirecting inherent challenges that are coded in the child's genes.

Imagine the relief in your family when you learn that by simply approaching little Johnny with a light touch and a

5 minute warning that he will be have to switch from one task to another, you will be able to avoid major power-struggles that have been plaguing your household.

Imagine teenager Sarah's newfound empowerment when she discovers the reason why she has a hard time focusing and getting overwhelmed and distracted. She can then take steps to change her environment on her

own and complete assignments more efficiently and effectively.

CHAPTER 17

Improving Relationships Through Face Reading

Face Reading is the relationship between physical features and personality. The science was developed in the 1930's by a California judge, who noticed a pattern between the characteristics of the face and the behavior of hundreds of people who appeared before him in court. So intrigued by these observations, he researched much of the information that was established in the 1800's and developed a system that reflected a 92% accuracy for personality and career assessment. Today the information is used for coaching, teaching, sales, relationships, career assessment, communication and personal development.

EXAMPLES OF TRAITS

Physical Insulation

This is determined by the thickness of a single hair strand. The finer the hair, the more sensitive that person is to their emotional and physical environment. Their feelings are easily hurt and are very sensitive to loud noises or unpleasant smells. They enjoy a quality lifestyle, camping out in the rough does not have great appeal; they would rather spend the night in a Bed and Breakfast. Whereas individuals with coarser hair have a love of the out doors. Enjoy louder music, rougher textures

and have stronger voices. They may see the finer haired person as being overly sensitive. In relationships we recommend the hair having similar thickness.

Tolerance

The distance between the eyes indicates an individual's level of tolerance. People who have close-set eyes are very focused on what they are doing. They are easily irritated, by interruptions, sloppy work or people not arriving on time for a meeting. If you were looking for someone who is very detailed, this trait along with pointed features would be ideal for the job. Individuals with wide set eyes are extremely tolerant, much more laid-back and open-minded. They enjoy the big picture and tend to take on too many things at once. Focus is their challenge.

Thinking Style

When looking at a person from the side profile notice whether the forehead slopes back quickly or is it more vertical? If it slopes back, this indicates the person is quick to think and respond. Very good in emergencies or where quick action is needed. Notice how many tennis or football players have sloped back foreheads. The vertical forehead are the sequential thinkers, they go through the learning process step-by-step and do not like to be rushed into making decisions. They like to 'think things through' before making a decision.

Body Balance

Are you short, medium or long legged? This determines if you do better in activities that are on or off your feet. How many times do you hear a person say, "I hate my desk job." Next time check their legs out they are probably short. These individuals have a hard time sitting still whereas the longer legged person is quite comfortable sitting down for long periods of time.

Emotional Expression

The larger the iris, the more that person expresses their emotions and feelings. Other people may see them as over reacting emotionally. They quickly feel and take on other people emotional needs, which can drain their energy. When the iris is very small, these individuals have a hard time expressing their feelings or emotions. They have feelings but have a harder time surfacing them.

Verbal Expression

The fuller the upper lip, the more that person loves to talk, which is an asset in story telling or giving a presentation. However, beware when asking these people for directions, they may end up giving you the tour. Whereas the thinner lipped people are usually very concise and to the point, they are turned off by lengthy verbose conversation. They give clear concise directions. At times the thinner lipped person may appear to be very brief, keep in mind this is not their intended message.

Samy Molcho